Snapchat Marketing for Business

An Entrepreneur's Guide to Snapchat Marketing Mastery for Business Success

Table of Contents

Chapter 1 – Social Media Marketing 4
Steps Involved in Social Marketing 6
Social Marketing and Advertising 7
Credibility and Importance of Social Marketing 9
Basic Marketing Principles 10
Stages of a Successful Social Marketing Effort 14
Examples of Successful Stages 15

Chapter 2 – Social Media Marketing Platforms 19
Social Media Marketing Platforms 20
Social Media Marketing Strategies 23
Laws of Social Media Marketing 33
Benefits of Social Media Marketing 36

Chapter 3 – Snapchat Marketing 43
Snapchat Marketing Guidelines and Tactics 45
Ways to Take Advantage of Snapchat 52
Best Marketing Brands on Snapchat 58

Conclusion 71

Chapter 2 – SEO Operation 72

Introduction

Have you ever wanted to learn to master the app, Snapchat? Right now and for the foreseeable future, Snapchat will be adding millions of users. Many project that it will soon outpace Facebook and Twitter as the most popular social media apps. To me, Snapchat is the future for social media as well as marketing, and I think companies are going to wise up to that fact soon.

This book covers social media as well, in terms of how it affects our lives and business. Understanding social media from the ground up is extremely important, and you will want to pay attention before we get into the nuances of Snapchat and the like.

By the end of reading this book, you will be able to understand the benefits of social media marketing, as well as how to use it affectively. Essentially, social media is all about connection and engagement, and it truly fulfills some of our greatest psychological needs.

Read on to discover how and why social media marketing started, and how we can use what we know to our best advantage. Thanks again for downloading "*Snapchat Marketing For Business: An Entrepreneur's Guide to Snapchat Marketing Mastery for Business Success*!"

Now let's get started!

Chapter 1 – Social Media Marketing

As an example of social media marketing, community groups do many different things to solve the issues that interest them. A group fighting child hunger might advocate free breakfasts at school, increased funding for WIC (Women and Infant Children), and more child-oriented legislation from the state senate. And to accomplish each of these goals, the group will spring into action: letter-writing campaigns, direct lobbying, and advertising in the media, to name just a few. Thousands of details and hard work by many people are usually involved in a successful initiative.

Looked at from a different perspective, however, it comes down to one thing. At the root of all of the group's work is one basic principle: *change people's behavior.* This is true not only for a child hunger campaign, but for almost any health or community development initiative. A coalition against violence wants people to stop committing acts of violence. A teen pregnancy initiative tries to put an end to children having children. And an organization for peace looks for the day when world peace is more than a lovely thought on holiday greeting cards. This concept of changing people's behavior is the basis of the principles that social marketing aims to do. It tries to enhance people's perception so that people's focus can be directed towards a certain term of thinking of an issue or a product. This usually entices people's sentimental values and individual thinking that reflects the product's image.

So what, exactly, is social marketing? In *Social Marketing Report*, it's defined as, "the application of commercial marketing techniques to social problems." It means to take the same principles used in selling goods—such as shoes, television shows, or pizza—to convince people to change their behavior. What does that mean? Well, instead of selling hamburgers, you're selling a life without heart attacks. Instead of convincing teenagers to buy blue jeans, you're convincing them to buy the advantages of postponing pregnancy. Of course, if you *are* selling blue jeans, you're still trying to influence behavior—you're convincing people they need to wear your jeans—either for comfort, or for style, or for value. So then, what is the difference between social marketing and commercial marketing? Commercial marketing tries to change people's behavior for the benefit of the marketer; social marketing tries to change people's behavior for the benefit of the consumer, or of society as a whole.

Steps Involved in Social Marketing

- Identify what behavior you want to change (for example, increase prenatal counseling among expectant mothers).

- Identify your audience: Whose behavior do you want to change? It may be that you want to change the behavior of several different groups; in that case, you may want to influence them in different ways to bring them closer to the desired behavior. Such groups are often separated, or segmented, by age, gender, level of education, or race.

- Identify the barriers to change: through interviews, surveys, focus groups or other methods, you'll want to find out what makes it difficult or unattractive for people to make these changes. Do pregnant women feel uncomfortable at the area clinic, or are they made to feel stupid when they talk to the doctor? Is the clinic too far away? Can they not take the time away from their jobs?

- Reduce the barriers to change. Plan ways to make it easier, more accessible, and more attractive. Can the clinic stay open longer hours? Can physicians and nurses be better trained to discuss problems with women? This step might even be taken a step farther. Your organization might provide incentives for making (and sustaining) changes. Mothers who come to the clinic regularly through their pregnancy might receive coupons for free baby food, for example.

- Pretest your ideas on a small number of people, then modify your plan according to your results.

- Publicize both the benefits of change, and also your efforts to make change easier in a way that will draw people to take advantage of your efforts. Let people know what you're doing to help them—the best program in the world won't be used if people don't know about it. And of course, people need to understand the benefits of the behavior change. A pregnant woman will probably want to do what's best for her child, but may not know that she needs extra iron during her pregnancy. It's up to your organization to tell her.

Social Marketing and Advertising

A lot of people confuse social marketing with one of its components, advertising. But leaves are just one part of the tree—even when they're only part you can see.

Likewise, advertising is a very important part of social marketing, but it's still just a part.

Is that confusing? Well, look at the following messages:

- "This is your brain on drugs," said the Partnership for a Drug-Free America's advertisement a few years ago, while picturing an egg frying on a skillet. That was a memorable advertisement; but if that was all the Partnership had done, it wouldn't qualify as social marketing.

- "Don't mess with Texas," was a well-known anti-litter campaign in that state. But if the ad had been aired without additional trashcans placed around the state, or without having been directed at specific group of people in Texas (such as youth, or immigrants, or tourists); it would have been nothing more than a catchy slogan. It wouldn't have been social marketing.

- Smokey Bear and his admonition, "Only you can prevent forest fires," when seen alone on T.V., are again just an advertisement. But taken in context of all of the work done by the U.S. Forestry Service, the result that emerges is a social marketing campaign. Smokey is trying to change a particular behavior (being careless with fire); his message is targeted at a specific audience (six to ten year olds), and information he provides (on commercials, on the Internet and elsewhere) overcomes two major barriers to children being careful with fire: ignorance and also the scientific, "it's no fun" barrier. Further, the message is supported with information provided to parents at the campsites, making it more likely they will provide reinforcement to the message. That's social marketing. It uses targeted marketing, reinforcement, and it reduces barriers—three key elements missing from the two examples above.

Credibility and Importance of Social Marketing

The bad news is, there *is* a definite art to it—it's not all something you're born with, and it's not only common sense. After all, people get degrees in this stuff; and major corporations such as Nike or Coca-Cola spend millions of dollars to ensure that their marketing campaigns are state-of-the-art. That's why earlier in the overview, it was stated that the marketing prowess depends on one's creative intellect and skills. Now for the good news: first of all, it's a learnable trait. You may not have been born with phrases like *market segmentation* floating around in your head, but you can learn what they mean, and how to use them.

Second, it's scalable. Some campaigns are quite large, such as the National High Blood Pressure campaign. However, social marketing campaigns can also be quite a bit smaller. That is, you can do it on a local level, when you have limited resources. Just because your group doesn't run the Hyatt Regency, or hasn't resources anywhere in the same ballpark, that doesn't mean you can't take the same principles and put into effect the change that you want to see in your community.

There are three major advantages which suggest that social marketing is worthy of your consideration:

- It helps you reach the target audiences you want to reach.

- It helps you customize your message to those targeted audiences; and by doing so.

- It helps you create greater and longer-lasting behavior change in those audiences.

Social marketing is a good idea **because it works**.

Basic Marketing Principles

Before we discuss social marketing further, however, it's important to have a grasp on the principles of commercial marketing, since that is what it's based on.

As community health workers, or members of non-profit organizations, the idea might seem a bit odd. We're used to a completely different mindset. Terms like "marketing" may conjure up images of big business and corporate greed; they certainly don't make us think of programs to try to help our neighbors.

Even so, your neighbors may not be open to your ideas and programs right off the bat, and you may find yourself having to persuade them. This is what social marketing excels at. The idea may be new for you, or a complete change in how your perceive things. That change, however, may end up being the breath of air your organization needs to become even more effective in changing behavior.

The essence of all marketing can be summed up in what has been termed the "4 Ps." They are *product, price, place,* and *promotion.*

- Product — The product is what you are marketing. For social marketing, the "product" is a certain behavior you are trying to change. It might be ending child abuse and neglect, or stopping people from committing suicide, or convincing people to not throw trash on the ground—or any other behavior that members of your community want to modify.

- Price — How much will it cost a person to stop (or take on) a certain behavior? In social marketing, price isn't just a question of dollars and cents. It can also be a question of time (i.e., how long will it take me to find a trash can?), or how much of an effort a behavior change will take. A life-long smoker may be the first person to admit that smoking is an extremely expensive habit, but may still say the costs—in terms of effort, or possible weight gain, or nicotine withdrawal—are too high. He just can't quit.

A good social marketing plan, then will try to reduce these costs. An anti-litter campaign will try to place more trash cans around the city; a smoking cessation group might offer support groups to help with the effort, nutrition counseling to counteract weight gain, and nicotine patches to reduce the pangs of withdrawal.

- Place — How difficult is it to change the behavior? What barriers are preventing it? If you are selling blue jeans, you want to have them in stores across the country, not just in one small boutique in Snellville, Georgia. Otherwise, people in Oregon won't be able to get them, even if they want to.

Likewise, if you are "selling" teen pregnancy prevention, what barriers make it difficult to prevent those pregnancies? Can teenagers easily obtain birth control, or is it difficult for them to get hold of? Maybe there isn't a good teen clinic in town. Or if there is a clinic available, maybe it's all the way across town, and it's only open on weekdays until 4:00, making it difficult to get to without missing school.

Social marketing efforts make it easier to change behavior by making sure the necessary supports are not only available, but also easily accessible to the most people possible. The less people need to go out of their way to make a change, the more likely they are to make it.

- Promotion — Promotion is the last of the "4 Ps," and the one most easily associated with social marketing. Promotion is the advertising you do; be it in television commercials, letters to the editor, or red ribbons tied to car antennas.

Promoting your cause doesn't need to take a lot of money. It can also take place through less costly methods, such as good old-fashioned word of mouth. Convincing people through a one-on-one conversation can be just as effective at changing someone's point of view as the best made commercial, or even more so. (Think about it. Which would make you get a tetanus booster: a television commercial or a suggestion from your doctor?) Word of mouth is a highly desirable part of social marketing.

Stages of a Successful Social Marketing Effort

With that understanding of marketing in mind, let's turn now to the focal point of an effective campaign—the consumer. People will have different ideas and beliefs at different times. For example, among smokers, some may not believe smoking is that bad for them, others might understand the risks but not care, still others may not want to take the effort to stop smoking, and a final group of smokers may be actively trying to quit. A social marketing campaign will see all of these beliefs (and their related actions) as part of a continuum, and try to move people along to the next step.

The idea is that these changes won't happen overnight. Most people won't go immediately from believing smoking is "cool" and not really understanding the health risks to quitting right away. Instead, a social marketing campaign might start them thinking that it's not the best thing to do—and after that idea has had time to turn around in their head for a while, another part of the campaign will help them quit, and yet another part will help them remain smoke free.

How are these beliefs shaped and decisions made? Well, generally speaking, the following activities need to occur:

- Create awareness and interest
- Change attitudes and conditions
- Motivate people to *want* to change their behavior
- Empower people to act
- Prevent backsliding

Examples of Successful Stages

In much of Africa, women have traditionally had many, many children; in such countries as Nigeria, the average woman might bear as many as 12 children during her lifetime. A social marketing message that has been widely disseminated, then, is *have fewer children*. This message has been geared towards the goals of increasing women's health, and decreasing overpopulation and famine.

- Create awareness and interest. The recipient must *get the message,* literally. You have to get the recipient's attention. The message needs to be brought to women all over the country, including village women who are generally illiterate, speak only a local dialect, and who often don't have access to television or radios. Also, the recipient must *understand* the message. Not only does the message need to be conveyed to the women in a language they understand; it needs to make sense for their lives as well. For women in Africa, wealth and status have traditionally been tied up in how many children they bear. The idea of having fewer children hasn't made sense because doing so would have hurt their standing in the community, even if it would improve their health.

- Change attitudes and conditions. The recipient has to *develop a positive attitude* or *positive frame of mind* about the behavior in question. With effective social marketing, African women might come to think, "Maybe it is better to have fewer children."

- Motivate people to want to change their behavior. The recipient has to *form an intention* to act on the basis of that attitude. It's not enough to just convince people that something is a good idea. A leap needs to be made from thinking something is a "good idea" to the stage of "I will do that." Think about it—how many of us think it would be a really good idea to cut down on our fat intake, or get up at 5:00 a.m. to exercise? Social marketing helps people move from attitude to intention, and beyond. For African women, this might mean taking the leap to find out about birth control or planning to postpone intercourse.

- Empowering people to act. The recipient has to act, i.e., convert that intention into action. A woman or her partner needs to go to the clinic and get the birth control, and use it.

- Prevent backsliding. Often, the recipient's action must be *followed by reinforcement*, by the provision of some benefit for having acted, so that the desired action will be repeated. How is her life better in a meaningful way for having fewer children? Will her friends and family improve? Will she have more money? Can she go to school? Is she healthier than her neighbors?

As we mentioned above, not every person will be at the same place on the continuum. It's like they are at different points on a bridge, spanning from attention to action.

Social marketing is a concept that's fairly new to the health and development field. Nonetheless, it's an idea that shows immense promise, and can give you an excellent framework through which your organization can do what you have set out to do: help individuals and society as our whole live better lives. Modern business marketplace has an integral place for business promotion when it comes to Social Marketing in such a competitive marketplace. Hence, with technological advances in modern times, it would be unwise not to use these advances in order to market products over a social scale. This is where social marketing plays an important role, and the role it is most used in is in social media. Hence, giving birth to Social Media Marketing.

Chapter 2 – Social Media Marketing Platforms

Social media marketing, or SMM, is a form of internet marketing that implements various social media networks in order to achieve marketing communication and branding goals. Social media marketing primarily covers activities involving social sharing of content, videos, and images for marketing purposes, as well as paid social media advertising. Most of these social media platforms have their own built-in data analytics tools, which enable companies to track the progress, success, and engagement of ad campaigns. Social media marketing programs usually center on efforts to create content that attracts attention and encourages readers to share it with their social networks. A corporate message spreads from user to user and presumably resonates because it appears to come from a trusted, third-party source, as opposed to the brand or company itself. Hence, this form of marketing is driven by word-of-mouth, meaning it results in earned media rather than paid media. Social media has become a platform that is easily accessible to anyone with internet access. Increased communication for organizations fosters brand awareness and often, improved customer service. Additionally, social media serves as a relatively inexpensive platform for organizations to implement marketing campaigns. Companies address a range of stakeholders through social media marketing including current and potential customers, current and potential employees, journalists, bloggers, and the general public. On a strategic level, social media marketing includes the management of the implementation of a marketing campaign, governance, setting the scope (e.g. more active or passive use) and the establishment of a firm's desired social media "culture" and "tone". To use social media effectively, firms should learn to allow customers and Internet users to post user-generated content (e.g., online comments, product reviews, etc.), also known as "earned media", rather than use marketer-prepared advertising copy. While social media marketing is often associated with companies, as of 2016, a range of not-for-profit organizations and government organizations are engaging in social media marketing of their programs or services.

Social Media Marketing Platforms

Social networking websites allow individual, businesses and other organizations to interact with one another and build relationships and communities online. When companies join these social channels, consumers can interact with them directly. That interaction can be more personal to users than traditional methods of outbound marketing and advertising. Social networking sites act as word of mouth or more accurately, e-word of mouth. The Internet's ability to reach billions across the globe has given online word of mouth a powerful voice and far reach. The ability to rapidly change buying patterns and product or service acquisition and activity to a growing number of consumers is defined as an influence network. Social networking sites and blogs allow followers to "retweet" or "repost" comments made by others about a product being promoted, which occurs quite frequently on some social media sites. By repeating the message, the user's connections are able to see the message, therefore reaching more people. Because the information about the product is being put out there and is getting repeated, more traffic is brought to the product/company.

Social networking websites are based on building virtual communities that allow consumers to express their needs, wants and values, online. Social media marketing then connects these consumers and audiences to businesses that share the same needs, wants, and values. Through social networking sites, companies can keep in touch with individual followers. This personal interaction can instill a feeling of loyalty into followers and potential customers. Also, by choosing whom to follow on these sites, products can reach a very narrow target audience. Social networking sites also include much information about what products and services prospective clients might be interested in. Through the use of new semantic analysis technologies, marketers can detect buying signals, such as content shared by people and questions posted online. An understanding of buying signals can help sales people target relevant prospects and marketers run micro-targeted campaigns.

To integrate social networks into their marketing strategies, companies have to develop a marketing model. In a marketing model based on social networks is provided. The model includes the following steps:

- Selection of the potential social networks to use;

- Setting out a financial plan (regarding hiring social media brand managers or consultants);

- Designing or modifying organizational structures to manage the social network in the companies' market (this may involve adding a social media unit to an existing marketing branch or creating a new social media branch);

- Selection of target markets;

- Selection of the products, services, brands or company messages which will be promoted;

- Performance measures for the social media strategy such as evaluation, data analytics, etc.

In 2014, over 80% of business executives identified social media as an integral part of their business. Business retailers have seen 133% increases in their revenues from social media marketing.

Social Media Marketing Strategies

There are two basic strategies for engaging the social media as marketing tools:

Passive Approach

Social media can be a useful source of market information and a way to hear customer perspectives. Blogs, content communities, and forums are platforms where individuals share their reviews and recommendations of brands, products, and services. Businesses are able to tap and analyze the customer voices and feedback generated in social media for marketing purposes; in this sense the social media is a relatively inexpensive source of market intelligence which can be used by marketers and managers to track and respond to consumer-identified problems and detect market opportunities. For example, the Internet erupted with videos and pictures of iPhone 6 "bend test" which showed that the coveted phone could be bent by hand pressure. The so-called "bend gate" controversy created confusion amongst customers who had waited months for the launch of the latest rendition of the iPhone. However, Apple promptly issued a statement saying that the problem was extremely rare and that the company had taken several steps to make the mobile device's case stronger and robust. Unlike traditional market research methods such as surveys, focus groups, and data mining which are time-consuming and costly, and which take weeks or even months to analyze, marketers can use social media to obtain 'live' or "real time" information about consumer behavior and viewpoints on a company's brand or products. This can be useful in the highly dynamic, competitive fast-paced and global marketplace of the 2010s.

Active Approach

Social media can be used not only as public relations and direct marketing tools but also as communication channels targeting very specific audiences with social media influencers and social media personalities and as effective customer engagement tools. Technologies predating social media, such as broadcast TV and newspapers can also provide advertisers with a fairly targeted audience, given that an ad placed during a sports game broadcast or in the sports section of a newspaper is likely to be read by sports fans. However, social media websites can target niche markets even more precisely. Using digital tools such as Google Ad-Sense, advertisers can target their ads to very specific demographics, such as people who are interested in social entrepreneurship, political activism associated with a particular political party, or video gaming. Google Ad-Sense does this by looking for keywords in social media user's online posts and comments. It would be hard for a TV station or paper-based newspaper to provide ads that are this targeted (though not impossible, as can be seen with "special issue" sections on niche issues, which newspapers can use to sell targeted ads).

However, there are certain strategic steps that a company may adapt in order to enhance its social perception and promotion through social media marketing.

1. Identify Business Goals

Every piece of your social media strategy serves the goals you set. You simply can't move forward without knowing what you're working toward.

Look closely at your company's overall needs and decide how you want to use social media to contribute to reaching them.

You'll undoubtedly come up with several personalized goals, but there are a few that all companies should include in their strategy—increasing brand awareness, retaining customers and reducing marketing costs are relevant to everyone. I suggest you choose two primary goals and two secondary goals to focus on. Having too many goals distracts you and you'll end up achieving none.

2. Set Marketing Objectives

Goals aren't terribly useful if you don't have specific parameters that define when each is achieved. For example, if one of your primary goals is generating leads and sales, how many leads and sales do you have to generate before you consider that goal a success?

Marketing objectives define how you get from Point A (an unfulfilled goal) to Point B (a successfully fulfilled goal). You can determine your objectives with the S–M–

A-R-T approach: Make your objectives specific, measurable, achievable, relevant and time-bound.

Using our previous example, if your goal is to generate leads and sales, a specific marketing objective may be to increase leads by 50%. In order to measure your progress, choose which analytics and tracking tools you need to have in place. Setting yourself up for failure is never a good idea. If you set an objective of increasing sales by 1,000%, it's doubtful you'll meet it. Choose objectives you can achieve, given the resources you have. You've taken the time to refine your goals so they're relevant to your company, so extend that same consideration to your objectives. If you want to get support from your C-level executives, ensure your objectives are relevant to the company's overall vision.

Attaching a timeframe to your efforts is imperative. When do you intend to achieve your goal(s)? Next month? By the end of this year?

Your objective of increasing leads by 50% may be specific, measurable, achievable and relevant, but if you don't set a deadline for achieving the goal, your efforts, resources and attention may be pulled in other directions.

3. Identify Ideal Customers

If a business is suffering from low engagement on their social profiles, it's usually because they don't have an accurate ideal customer profile. Buyer personas help you define and target the right people, in the right places, at the right times with the right messages.

When you know your target audience's age, occupation, income, interests, pains, problems, obstacles, habits, likes, dislikes, motivations and objections, then it's easier and cheaper to target them on social or any other media. The more specific you are, the more conversions you're going to get out of every channel you use to promote your business.

4. Research Competition

When it comes to social media marketing, researching your competition not only keeps you apprised of their activity, it gives you an idea of what's working so you can integrate those successful tactics into your own efforts. Start by compiling a list of at least 3–5 main competitors. Search which social networks they're using and analyze their content strategy. Look at their number of fans or followers, posting frequency and time of day. Also pay attention to the type of content they're posting and its context (humorous, promotional, etc.) and how they're responding to their fans.

The most important activity to look at is engagement. Even though page admins are the only ones who can calculate engagement rate on a particular update, you can get a good idea of what they're seeing.

For example, let's say you're looking at a competitor's last 20–30 Facebook updates. Take the total number of engagement activities for those posts and divide it by the page's total number of fans. (Engagement activity includes likes, comments, shares, etc.)

You can use that formula on all of your competitors' social profiles (e.g., on Twitter you can calculate retweets and favorites). Keep in mind that the calculation is meant to give you a general picture of how the competition is doing so you can compare how you stack up against each other.

5. Choose Channels and Tactics

Many businesses create accounts on every popular social network without researching which platform will bring the most return. You can avoid wasting your time in the wrong place by using the information from your buyer personas to determine which platform is best for you. If your prospects or customers tell you they spend 40% of their online time on Facebook and 20% on Twitter, you know which primary and secondary social networks you should focus on.

When your customers are using a specific network, that's where you need to be—not everywhere else. Your tactics for each social channel rely on your goals and objectives, as well as the best practices of each platform. For example, if your goal is increasing leads and your primary social network is Facebook, some effective tactics are investing in Facebook advertising or promotion campaigns to draw more attention to your lead magnets.

6. Create a Content Strategy

Content and social media have a symbiotic relationship: Without great content social media is meaningless and without social media nobody will know about your content. Use them together to reach and convert your prospects.

There are three main components to any successful social media content strategy: type of content, time of posting and frequency of posting.

The type of content you should post on each social network relies on form and context. Form is how you present that information—text only, images, links, video, etc.

Context fits with your company voice and platform trends. Should your content be funny, serious, highly detailed and educational or something else?

There are many studies that give you a specific time when you should post on social media. However, I suggest using those studies as guidelines rather than hard rules. Remember, your audience is unique, so you need to test and figure out the best time for yourself.

Posting frequency is as important as the content you share. You don't want to annoy your fans or followers, do you?

Finding the perfect frequency is crucial because it could mean more engagement for your content or more unlikes and unfollows. Use Facebook Insights to see when your fans are online and engaging with your content.

7. Allocate Budget and Resources

To budget for social media marketing, look at the tactics you've chosen to achieve your business goals and objectives. Make a comprehensive list of the tools you need (e.g., social media monitoring, email marketing and CRM), services you'll outsource (e.g., graphic design or video production) and any advertising you'll purchase. Next to each, include the annual projected cost so you can have a high-level view of what you're investing in and how it affects your marketing budget.

Many businesses establish their budget first, and then select which tactics fit that budget. I take the opposite approach. I establish a strategy first, and then determine the budget that fits that strategy.

If your strategy execution fees exceed your budget estimate, prioritize your tactics according to their ROI timeframe. The tactics with the fastest ROI (e.g., advertising and social referral) take priority because they generate instant profit you can later invest into long-term tactics (fan acquisition, quality content creation or long-term engagement).

8. Assign Roles
Knowing who's responsible for what increases productivity and avoids confusion and overlapping efforts. Things may be a bit messy in the beginning, but with time team members will know their roles and what daily tasks they're responsible for.

When everyone knows his or her role, it's time to start planning the execution process. You can either plan daily or weekly. I don't advise putting a monthly plan together because lots of things will come up and you may end up wasting time adapting to the new changes. You can use tools like Basecamp or ActiveCollab to manage your team and assign tasks to each member.

These tools save you tons of time and help you stay organized.

Laws of Social Media Marketing

The strategies of social media marketing are applicable only when certain principles are followed, certain laws that have thorough path to promotional success. These laws help as a basis of promotional operations of a business to enhance the marketing prowess of the business, or the brand. Leveraging the power of content and social media marketing can help elevate your audience and customer base in a dramatic way. But getting started without any previous experience or insight could be challenging.

It's vital that you understand social media marketing fundamentals. From maximizing quality to increasing your online entry points, abiding by these 10 laws will help build a foundation that will serve your customers, your brand and — perhaps most importantly — your bottom line.

1. The Law of Listening
Success with social media and content marketing requires more listening and less talking. Read your target audience's online content and join discussions to learn what's important to them. Only then can you

create content and spark conversations that add value rather than clutter to their lives.

2. The Law of Focus

It's better to specialize than to be a jack-of-all-trades. A highly-focused social media and content marketing strategy intended to build a strong brand has a better chance for success than a broad strategy that attempts to be all things to all people.

3. The Law of Quality

Quality trumps quantity. It's better to have 1,000 online connections who read, share and talk about your content with their own audiences than 10,000 connections who disappear after connecting with you the first time.

4. The Law of Patience

Social media and content marketing success doesn't happen overnight. While it's possible to catch lightning in a bottle, it's far more likely that you'll need to commit to the long haul to achieve results.

5. The Law of Compounding

If you publish amazing, quality content and work to build your online audience of quality followers, they'll share it with their own audiences on Twitter, Facebook, LinkedIn, their own blogs and more.

This sharing and discussing of your content opens new entry points for search engines like Google to find it in keyword searches. Those entry points could grow to hundreds or thousands of more potential ways for people to find you online.

6. The Law of Influence

Spend time finding the online influencers in your market who have quality audiences and are likely to be interested in your products, services and business. Connect with those people and work to build relationships with them.

If you get on their radar as an authoritative, interesting source of useful information, they might share your content with their own followers, which could put you and your business in front of a huge new audience.

7. The Law of Value

If you spend all your time on the social Web directly promoting your products and services, people will stop listening. You must add value to the conversation. Focus less on conversions and more on creating amazing content and developing relationships with online influencers. In time, those people will become a powerful catalyst for word-of-mouth marketing for your business.

8. The Law of Acknowledgment

You wouldn't ignore someone who reaches out to you in person so don't ignore them online. Building relationships is one of the most important parts of social media marketing success, so always acknowledge every person who reaches out to you.

9. The Law of Accessibility

Don't publish your content and then disappear. Be available to your audience. That means you need to consistently publish content and participate in conversations. Followers online can be fickle and they won't hesitate to replace you if you disappear for weeks or months.

10. The Law of Reciprocity

You can't expect others to share your content and talk about you if you don't do the same for them. So, a portion of the time you spend on social media should be focused on sharing and talking about content published by others.

Benefits of Social Media Marketing

Social media has developed a reputation by some for being a passing marketing interest, and therefore, an unprofitable one due to its quick advent. The statistics, however, illustrate a different picture. According to

Hubspot, 92% of marketers in 2014 claimed that social media marketing was important for their business, with 80% indicating their efforts increased traffic to their websites. And according to Social Media Examiner, 97% of marketers are currently participating in social media—but 85% of participants aren't sure what social media tools are the best to use.

This demonstrates a huge potential for social media marketing to increase sales, but a lack of understanding on how to achieve those results. Here's a look at just some of the ways social media marketing can improve your business:

1. Increased Brand Recognition. Every opportunity you have to syndicate your content and increase your visibility is valuable. Your social media networks are just new channels for your brand's voice and content. This is important because it simultaneously makes you easier and more accessible for new customers, and makes you more familiar and recognizable for existing customers. For example, a frequent Twitter user could hear about your company for the first time only after stumbling upon it in a newsfeed. Or, an otherwise apathetic customer might become better acquainted with your brand after seeing your presence on multiple networks.

2. Improved brand loyalty. According to a report published by Texas Tech University, brands who engage on social media channels enjoy higher loyalty from their customers. The report concludes "Companies should take advantage of the tools social media gives them when it comes to connecting with their audience. A strategic and open social media plan could prove influential in morphing consumers into being brand loyal." Another study published by Convince&Convert found that 53% of Americans who follow brands in social are more loyal to those brands.

3. More Opportunities to Convert. Every post you make on a social media platform is an opportunity for customers to convert. When you build a following, you'll simultaneously have access to new customers, recent customers, and old customers, and you'll be able to interact with all of them. Every blog post, image, video, or comment you share is a chance for someone to react, and every reaction could lead to a site visit, and eventually a conversion. Not every interaction with your brand results in a conversion, but every positive interaction increases the likelihood of an eventual conversion. Even if your click-through rates are low, the sheer number of opportunities you have on social media is significant. And as I pointed out in my article, "The Four Elements of Any Action, And How

To Use Them In Your Online Marketing Initiative," "opportunity" is the first element of any action.

4. Higher conversion rates. Social media marketing results in higher conversion rates in a few distinct ways. Perhaps the most significant is its humanization element; the fact that brands becomes more humanized by interacting in social media channels. Social media is a place where brands can act like people do, and this is important because people like doing business with other people; not with companies.

Additionally, studies have shown that social media has a 100% higher lead-to-close rate than outbound marketing, and a higher number of social media followers tends to improve trust and credibility in your brand, representing social proof. As such, simply building your audience in social media can improve conversion rates on your existing traffic.

5. Higher Brand Authority. Interacting with your customers regularly is a show of good faith for other customers. When people go to compliment or brag about a product or service, they turn to social media. And when they post your brand name, new audience members will want to follow you for updates. The more people that are talking about you on social media, the more valuable and authoritative your brand will seem

to new users. Not to mention, if you can interact with major influencers on Twitter or other social networks, your visible authority and reach will skyrocket.

6. Increased Inbound Traffic. Without social media, your inbound traffic is limited to people already familiar with your brand and individuals searching for keywords you currently rank for. Every social media profile you add is another path leading back to your site, and every piece of content you syndicate on those profiles is another opportunity for a new visitor. The more quality content you syndicate on social media, the more inbound traffic you'll generate, and more traffic means more leads and more conversions.

7. Decreased Marketing Costs. According to Hubspot, 84% of marketers found as little as six hours of effort per week were enough to generate increased traffic. Six hours is not a significant investment for a channel as large as social media. If you can lend just one hour a day to developing your content and syndication strategy, you could start seeing the results of your efforts. Even paid advertising through Facebook and Twitter is relatively cheap (depending on your goals, of course). Start small and you'll never have to worry about going over budget—once you get a better feel for what to expect, you can increase your budget and increase your conversions correspondingly.

8. Better Search Engine Rankings. SEO is the best way to capture relevant traffic from search engines, but the requirements for success are always changing. It's no longer enough to regularly update your blog, ensure optimized title tags and Meta descriptions, and distribute links pointing back to your site. Google and other search engines may be calculating their rankings using social media presence as a significant factor, because of the fact that strong brands almost always use social media. As such, being active on social media could act as a "brand signal" to search engines that your brand is legitimate, credible, and trustworthy. That means, if you want to rank for a given set of keywords, having a strong social media presence could be almost mandatory.

9. Richer Customer Experiences. Social media, at its core, is a communication channel like email or phone calls. Every customer interaction you have on social media is an opportunity to publicly demonstrate your customer service level and enrich your relationship with your customers. For example, if a customer complains about your product on Twitter, you can immediately address the comment, apologize publicly, and take action to make it right. Or, if a customer compliments you, you can thank them and recommend

additional products. It's a personal experience that lets customers know you care about them.

10. Improved Customer Insights. Social media also gives you an opportunity to gain valuable information about what your customers are interested in and how they behave, via social listening. For example, you can monitor user comments to see what people think of your business directly. You can segment your content syndication lists based on topic and see which types of content generate the most interest—and then produce more of that type of content. You can conversions based on different promotions posted on various social media channels and eventually find a perfect combination to generate revenue.

The longer you wait, the more you have to lose. Social media marketing, when done right, can lead to more customers, more traffic, and more conversions, and its here to stay.

Chapter 3 – Snapchat Marketing

All the above parameters of social media marketing and social marketing as a whole have an integral part in business promotion through social media means. Each different platform of social media has distinct feature, but the functionality in marketing is similar. Every platform uses interaction as an intuitive prospect in order to promote its brand, or product or service, using a brief, socially affluent language that is attractive to the viewer. However, the distinct medium of media that Snapchat uses makes it difficult to relate to other platforms of social media used for marketing.

Snapchat launched in 2011 and rocketed into the mainstream last year after Facebook tried and failed to kill it, but brands have been slow to embrace the platform. Snapchat is a mobile-only messaging app that allows users to send a photo or video "snap" that automatically deletes after being viewed. The sender can choose the amount of time the snap can be viewed, from one to ten seconds, and the message disappears forever.

According to Snapchat's internal data, there are more than 60% of U.S. smartphone users aged 13 to 34 that are Snapchatters. If reaching out to 13 to 34-year-olds is your goal, Snapchat is the best social platform to invest in. 13 to 34-year-olds love Snapchat because of three factors:

- Perspective. Snaps provide users and their friends a more personal avenue to show how they see the world.

- Real-time stories. Snapchat stories are raw, updated in real-time, and can only be viewed within 24 hours.

- Self-expression. Through snaps, users can show the world who they are in the exact moment.

Although Snapchat's majority of viewers come from the younger generation, there 12% of 35 to 54-year-olds and 2% of 55+-year-olds that are also Snapchatters. In fact, every single day, there are a total of more than 7 billion views on Snapchat. And, there are nearly 100 million active Snapchatters that use the application every day.

What makes Snapchat different from other social media platforms is the ability to form a personal connection with the recipient. Unlike the other social networks where the posts are public, a snap is delivered and comes across as being tailored specifically to the recipient, even though the snap itself could have been sent to an entire group of people!

It gives your company the ability to form a personal connection with someone. Snaps can't be forwarded or shared to others, so it makes one feel special to receive a snap.

Snapchat Marketing Guidelines and Tactics

Utilizing the Snapchat app to connect with a buyer persona can be tricky. It's worth noting that Snapchat puts a limit on how long its videos and photos are available for on the app. For instance, a video or photo will disappear as soon as a few seconds go by, never to be seen again by the recipient. This means that marketers need to make the most of every second they get on the app, which requires a certain amount of strategy.

Understanding Your Audience

Even if your target audience is a group of executives, it's important to grasp the environment of Snapchat. Since the beginning, Snapchat has been an app that encourages casual communication through the use of videos and photos. People take pictures of their meals, vacations, and daily activities to share with friends – they aren't typically documenting professional behavior.

That being said, it's critical to observe the overall casualness of the app. When your marketing team is creating a strategy for Snapchat, you need to settle on a tone of voice that will be used across the board. Ideally, the language you use should be easy-to-understand, and your posts should have a sense of fun. For instance, think about incorporating the drawing function on Snapchat that allows you to add edits to your photos. Doing so will make your team seem more personable and approachable – all added bonuses when attempting to connect with your audience.

If you're just starting out on Snapchat, take some time to do your homework. Browse through other accounts and follow other people to get a better idea of how they use the app.

Embrace it as Ephemeral

If you want to use Snapchat as a platform for your marketing campaign, you need to think of its time-limit feature as an opportunity, not a problem. The reason Snapchat has piqued the interest of so many young phone holders is because the time limit captures their attention, holds it, and then leaves them laughing, scratching their heads or speechless. Nonprofits on this platform need to do the same thing with their marketing campaign.

What I find interesting about self destructing content is how this plays into problems that have emerged around the nature of publishing content on the web. The internet has provided the public with the unique opportunity for people like me to publish freely and thereby providing readers access to information that was otherwise unavailable, but this freedom has created new challenges.

One of those is managing information. Part of the appeal of a platform like Snapchat is that it is ephemeral, and that we don't have to sort through tons of messages.

Focus on Relationship Building

Reaching a smaller engaged audience is more important for nonprofits than a massive disengaged audience.

It's not how many followers you have, it's how many care. It's not width, its depth. It's not how many impressions you get, it's how engaged they are with your cause.

Snapchat is an ephemeral, one-to-one experience which yields high engagement allowing nonprofits to deepen relationships with supporters because of the perceived intimacy of the platform.

Applying this theory to non-profit organizations, sending donor specific Snaps could increase donor involvement with projects as they can see first-hand the impact their support has on a project or sharing behind the scenes images of the programs you are delivering and the work you do. Providing this type of intimate access will make supporters feel closer to your cause.

Embracing the Time Limit

While some may perceive the self-destructive nature of Snapchat to be a hurdle, marketers can do wonders with this aspect of the app. More specifically, Technorati states that this can give you opportunity to offer teasers to your followers on Snapchat. Because videos and photos only exist for a few seconds, you can use Snapchat to give people a preview of an upcoming product or service that your company may be offering.

You can also use Snapchat to create contests. For instance, you can ask other users to send you pictures of them using your product and offer a reward to those who do. The trick to getting the most leverage out of Snapchat is ensuring that you are always looking for ways to engage with your customers. Doing so can keep people coming back for more, giving you additional opportunities to roll out your marketing strategy.

Get Going with Video

Snapchat is not just all about self-destructing photos - videos are a key component of the website as well. Although they also disappear once they have been viewed, marketers can use them to reach out to people who are interested in getting a sneak peek of their office culture, product production, and everything in between.

Marketing teams can use video to provide more valuable content to their followers. Although they say a picture is worth a thousand words, you can actually verbalize the message you're trying to convey to your audience through a video. More importantly, you don't need to be a professional to make a splash. Remember: Snapchat is all about being casual and relatable.

Portraying Your Personality

As it goes with any type of social media, Snapchat gives you a chance to portray the true intentions and mission of your company, whether it involves providing a service or a valuable product. Ideally, the media that you share over the app should give people a better idea of your business and what you have to offer. You should always be working to inject personality into your photos and videos to help people connect to your brand on a "human-like" level; a concept I covered in my article, "Why It's Important to Humanize Your Brand on Social Media."

Snapchat, like Twitter, Facebook, and Google+ before it, will likely develop additional features as it grows. One of the most recent additions was the launch of Snapchat Stories, a feature which enables brands to build and string together a narrative over the course of a day. Stories can be viewed as many times before the 24 hours is up and then they disappear. Clips are removed piece by piece as they reach the time limit and newer ones are added to the end of the story cycle.

The ability of Snapchat Stories to build a daylong narrative opens the door for creative uses of Snapchat by brands. Brands can now create a connected and engaging narrative for users, instead of relying on one-off snaps. Much like Vine brought about flipbook-style videos for brands; Snapchat provides a medium for content that tells a connected story that doesn't get disrupted by the content of other accounts and allows for a narrative thread to be built.

This could be an interesting method to show progress and development over the course of a 24-hour cycle. Especially in organizations that focus on rehabilitation or emergency relief, 24 hours of storytelling could have a significant impact. Use Snapchat to show off more than just content, but what happens behind the scenes. Ask different people at your company to contribute to your Snapchat efforts to add some flavor. Over time, you'll notice a difference in how quickly your following grows.

Snapchat at a Glance

If you're still unsure of whether there's any value to using Snapchat for marketing purposes, consider some statistics. There are approximately 26 million users in the U.S., and about 400 million snaps are sent out each day. If you aren't using Snapchat in your marketing strategy, you could be missing out on the opportunity to connect with dozens of people who fit into your target audience. However, there's more to bridging the gap than just downloading the app.

By taking these insights into account, you can ensure that you're unlocking all of the potential of Snapchat.

Ways to Take Advantage of Snapchat

1. Stage an Influencer Reveal

Global fast-food giant McDonald's (username: McDonalds) isn't just about a famous redheaded clown selling toys with a meal. Professional athletes like LeBron James gave users a behind-the-scenes look at the rollout of the new bacon clubhouse sandwich. Although McDonald's didn't share the results of the promotion, it went well enough to continue. The promotion was pushed to Twitter where users were asked to follow back. To date, McDonald's has over 3 million followers on Twitter.

Takeaway: You can apply this same philosophy with Snapchat to give your customers a look at what goes on behind the scenes at your company. Even if your marketing budget is only a fraction of what McDonald's is, buyers still like feeling as if they know the story behind your company.

2. Support an Account Takeover

The popular young women's clothing retailer Wet Seal (username: wetseal) launched a Snapchat campaign, which was quickly taken over by a Snapchatter named MsMeghanMakeup.

Meghan has over 300,000 followers and her influence was quickly felt as a halo effect over Wet Seal's campaign. The boost propelled the clothier to 9,000 connections in two weeks and over 250,000 views of the holiday "story." Wet Seal was named winner of the 6th Annual Shorty Awards, which honors the best in social media.

Takeaway: To get your message seen, you can let an influential Snapchat user take over your account. You may not have connections with 300K+ followers, but even local authorities with hundreds or thousands of fans can improve your Snapchat reach.

3. Share Promo Codes

Frozen yogurt chain 16 Handles (username: love16handles) used Snapchat's instant photo feature to amass followers and promote their frozen treats. They were also among the first brands to use Snapchat for coupon offers.

The yogurt company earned new customers by promoting specific store locations and times, and when people snapped photos of themselves or their friends eating 16 Handles yogurt, they instantly received a coupon code for between 16% and 100% off. The catch: They only had 10 seconds to show the cashier.

Takeaway: You can get your followers involved with Snapchat-exclusive coupon codes or other exclusive promos. Make it fun and your brand's reach is sure to grow!

4. Give VIP Access

In the past, it took several weeks for photos from New York Fashion Week to trickle down from photographers to magazines, and then from newsstands to consumers. Now, with Snapchat, followers can watch the fashions unfold almost instantly.

Lucky Magazine's editor-in-chief, fashion brand Refinery 29, and many others shared snaps of models strutting down the catwalk, allowing them to deliver images of the iconic fashion show to people in ways never dreamed of before.

Takeaway: You can use Snapchat to give your followers a VIP look at your events and promotions that they'll likely never have a chance to attend in person. It's a fun, easy way to bring new life to established events.

5. Feature Your Followers

Mobile and online food ordering brand GrubHub (username: grubhub) launched its first Snapchat campaign in 2013, becoming a finalist in the 7th Annual Shorty Awards. They featured their own weekly content, stories gathered from user-generated content, giveaways, and promotions.

The results included a 20% increase in followers after the launch of the Snapchat giveaway. The campaign was one of many factors that contributed to its Wall Street debut in a public offering.

Takeaway: Don't let your Snapchat feed become too self-serving. Make your feed about your followers, offer them value, and engage them in the content creation process.

6. Demo Your Product

The world's biggest online retailer, Amazon (username: amazon), used Snapchat to give a personality and voice to Alexa, the company's female-voiced Echo speaker. In a clever use of social media, Amazon employed Snapchat to give clarity to the product, which confused consumers when it launched, as well as to promote Echo.

Thanks to its campaign, Amazon gained 6,100 mentions in just four hours. It demonstrated that Echo was off to a promising start.

Takeaway: If your brand releases new technology or products, use Snapchat as a guide for new customers.

It's a clever way to use Snapchat and introduce new products and engage with potential customers.

7. Partner with Influencers

Sour Patch Kids (username: sourpatchsnaps) is a big hit among the Snapchat demographic, which is also the company's target audience. Mondelez, the company behind the brand, worked with social media personality Logan Paul to produce content for chats.

Over the course of five days, Paul documented childish pranks pulled on unsuspecting people, with the pranks dubbed "sweet" or "sour" to highlight the brand's flavors. The brand encouraged fans to post and promote the next story. The campaign earned Sour Patch Kids 120,000 new Snapchat followers.

Takeaway: Work with an influencer whose follower base is similar to yours to share snaps that coincide with your brand's image. In the case of Sour Patch Kids, pranks and general silliness work well, both in terms of supporting the company's identity and in engaging the brand's followers. Your results may vary.

8. Address Relevant Issues

Historically, soap brand Dove (username: dove) appealed primarily to older women until it reached out to younger women using Snapchat. Over a period of two hours, 30 women chatted with psychologists and other ambassadors on Snapchat to share ideas and thoughts about self-esteem issues in a campaign to help boost young women's self-images.

The resulting snaps earned the brand 75 conversations and 130,000 views, leading Dove to say that they'll continue to measure both engagement and reach (conversations) as part of their campaign metrics going forward.

Takeaway: When it comes to Snapchat, don't be afraid to be real. Authenticity is essential on this hyper-social network.

9. Give Exclusive Previews

Business Insider reported that Acura (username: acura_insider) used Snapchat to build excitement for its racecar-like NSX. The automobile manufacturer sent 100 followers an exclusive preview of the new car. The first 100 new followers got this 6-second video of the speeding luxury car.

Acura was named a finalist in the 6th Annual Shorty Awards after successfully integrating Snapchat into its campaign. It created a lot of buzz for the car, which the company repurposed on Instagram, Vine, and Twitter.

Takeaway: You can reward your top customers and fans, too. Share exclusive information with a limited audience. It works whether you're an international auto manufacturer or a local "mom and pop" store.

10. Promote Events

iHeartRadio (username: iheartradio) used Snapchat to document and share its iHeartRadio Music Festival. For two days, the company gained a whopping 340 million impressions with the help of eager concertgoers who shared their experiences. The festival went viral on Snapchat.

Takeaway: Snapchat's ephemeral nature makes it the perfect fit to advertise limited-time-only events. Make it part of your next event to give fans the inside scoop.

Best Marketing Brands on Snapchat

Brands from every industry and with all manner of target demographic —from Sour Patch Kids to General Electric, and even HubSpot — are using Snapchat to connect with their fans and customers in a way that's low-cost, but highly personal and engaging. You'll notice the content they post on Snapchat isn't polished: it's raw and scrappy and fun. After all, Snapchat is all about letting your brand personality shine and relating to your target audience on a totally human level.

1. Sour Patch Kids

Many of the earliest adopters of Snapchat were teenagers, which gave the snack company, Modelez, an incentive to hop on the platform to promote its Sour Patch Kids candy brand.

In 2014, one of the company's major goals was to grow awareness among their core demographic: candy-loving teenagers in the United States. Because teenagers were reportedly spending more and more time on Snapchat, they decided to go there to create fun content teens could share with one another.

For their campaign "Real-Life Sour Patch Kids", the company teamed up with Logan Paul, a social media influencer and comedian, who spent five days recording pranks around New York City via Snapchat. It was a play off the brand tagline, "First they're sour, then they're sweet," as the pranks went from "sweet" at the beginning of the five days to more "sour" pranks as the week went on. Each month, new Stories were released showing the "Real Sour Patch Kids" acting like regular teenagers.

2. Everlane

The retail company Everlane was another early Snapchat adopter, but with an even more daring approach to the then-new social platform. In November 2015, they wrote this on their official blog: "We're here to make a bold claim. Snapchat is going to become the defacto social channel for Everlane. Over the past month, we've been testing it in small batches and we're in love."

Why did they love it so much? Because they found it was an even better way to showcase their radical approach to transparency than other social networks like Facebook.

"Facebook is a spot for updating our community and having one on one conversations," read the post. "But Snapchat is completely different. Snapchat gives us the chance to explore transparency in a completely new way. No fancy cameras. No editing. Just raw, live, footage. It's beautiful, and it's the platform for the modern generation."

Almost a year and a half later, they haven't turned back. The folks at Everlane use Snapchat as kind of a backstage pass into their ecommerce business, their events, and their culture. They use the Snapchat Story feature to create narratives around giving tours of their spaces, interviewing customers in their brick-and-mortar stores, and previewing new products. On #TransparencyTuesday, for example, they use Snapchat to record a walkthrough of their business or factories.

3. General Electric

Would you ever have guessed that General Electric, a multinational conglomerate corporation, would have an active and effective presence on Snapchat?

They've actually done an awesome job of using their platform to showcase their geeky personality and to encourage interest in science — something they've done well on other social media networks like Instagram and YouTube.

One of the best ways they use the platform is in a series in which they answer users' questions by explaining scientific concepts in a concise and fun way. For example, they recently shared some of their findings from their emoji science curriculum, which they established along with the National Science Foundation.

In addition to sharing their emoji science findings, they also encourage their Snapchat followers to interact directly with them. "Just add 'generalelectric' on

Snapchat, send us an emoji, and we'll send you some science," they wrote on their Tumblr.

GE's global director of innovation Sam Olstein said about Snapchat, "The disappearing nature of its content encourages repeat usage and provides us with a unique way to celebrate invention with an expanding community of young fans."

4. Gatorade

Gatorade doesn't have a Snapchat account of its own, but thanks to their epic sponsored lens Snapchat at the Super Bowl this year, we think they deserve a place on this list. (Note: A Snapchat lens is essentially a creative filter for your selfies. It's what you see when your friends send Snapchats of them puking rainbows.)

Here's what they did: When a football team wins a game, it's customary that the team dumps whatever sports drink is in the team cooler onto their coach's head. During the Super Bowl football game in 2016, the folks at PepsiCo-owned Gatorade released a genius Super Bowl Snapchat lens that let anyone give themselves a Gatorade bath, too.

To create the ad, the folks at Gatorade partnered with Snapchat to purchase a sponsored lens, which costs around $450,000 per sponsored lens on normal days and up to $750,000 on "peak days" like holidays and the Super Bowl.

Then, they had professional tennis player Serena Williams — whom Gatorade sponsors. The ad showed her getting virtually "dumped on" by a cooler of orange Gatorade, thanks to the lens. The company tweeted out a GIF of the Snapchat to get the momentum going, and by the end of the day, the sponsored lens had reportedly been viewed over 100 million times.

5. Warby Parker

At Warby Parker, Snapchat is used for a variety of topics: everything from showcasing their products ("Today on Snapchat, we try on our favorite Crystal frames in 15 seconds") to giving users a chance to hear from the company's co-founder Neil Blumenthal ("Our co-founder Neil Blumenthal is inside the secret room today. Tune in on Snapchat as he answers your questions!").

They have several Snapchat series, including a brand new one called "Desk Job." In one recent Snapchat Story, they featured one of their brand creative managers for his five desk essentials. Once a Snapchat Story is up, they promote them on Twitter, Instagram, and LinkedIn. (I noticed they didn't promote them on Facebook, which is probably a good thing: On

Facebook, it's important not be selective about what you publish and focus on quality, rather than quantity, of posts.)

6. GrubHub

GrubHub, also an early Snapchat adopter, has been putting out content on about a weekly basis since late 2013. But they use Snapchat a little differently than many of the folks on this list. Rather than producing one-way content, GrubHub focuses on building out an active community by sending out Snapchat messages that require responses, like exclusive coupons, contests, giveaways, and promotional codes.

They became one of the only brands to interact with almost every single Snapchat message sent to them by users, every single day of the week. By the end of 2014, GrubHub had earned the highest Snapchat score of any brand (53,668 at that time). This impressive commitment to engagement earned them a finalist spot in the Shorty Awards.

7. New York Times

The writers, editors, and other folks at *The New York Times* use Snapchat a little differently — sometimes poking fun at their misunderstanding of it, other times using it as a storytelling platform (and then analyzing it in writing later).

There was one Snapchat Story that was part of an analysis of what makes an objectively good Snapchat Story, which later culminated in this piece by Talya Minsberg. For the piece, she recruited journalists at *The Times* to participate in a mobile challenge to create an objectively good Snapchat Story.

So, what makes an objective good Snapchat Story? Minsberg says it's nearly impossible to define, but that "the best Snapchat stories generally are ones that tell a narrative in a personal, visual way that pulls in and keeps the viewer."

Another important take away from her piece is this: "Even Snapchat stories must uphold the same standards as anything else published by *The Times*. There are just more doodles and emojis in a Snapchat story than you would see in print!"

8. DJ Khaled

DJ Khaled may not be your typical brand, but he has single-handedly redefined the celebrity presence on Snapchat — and there's a lot brands can learn from him. In March 2016, less than a year after DJ Khaled had even heard of the app, it was reported that his

Snapchats were attracting around 3 million to 4 million viewers each.

What's his secret? First, his style of shooting videos is really effective. He likes to pair mundane daily routines — like putting on deodorant and watering his plants — with funny commentary and one-liners.

He has some mantras he repeats like "another one" and "bless up," which he's parlayed into some really expensive merchandise. He also likes to share "keys to wisdom," and even got his own geofilter on a road trip to Las Vegas for New Year's Eve (which anyone can do, by the way).

The combination of backstage pass-like topics, hilarious one-liners, and fun use of emojis makes Khaled's account very shareable and followable.

9. Domino's Pizza UK

The folks at Dominos Pizza have never been afraid to experiment with new social media channels. They were the first brand to use Tinder as part of a 2015 Valentine's Day campaign, and their "Tweet to Eat" campaign let fans order pizza via Twitter by sending a pizza emoji.

As for their global presence, their social media teams around the world have adopted the platform at different times. For example, Dominos Australia started using Snapchat as early as 2013, sending out Snapchat Stories that aligned with campaigns they were doing elsewhere on social media.

The U.K. team at Dominos Pizza didn't get on Snapchat until January 2016, but they started out with a pretty cool experiment that led to a lift in orders. On January 20, 2016, they turned their Snapchat Story into a short film, titled "Dough to Door."

The film follows the journey of a Dominos delivery driver who hits a few obstacles on his way to deliver a pizza to a customer — including an alien invasion. According to *The Drum,* they also showed a sequence of random letters throughout the film that amount to an exclusive discount code they could then use online.

The folks at Dominos found that the low-budget effort led to an increase in orders. "The film drove a lot more orders then we would've expected even though it wasn't really a massive driver for us," Nick Dutch, Dominos' head of digital strategy, told *Business Insider.*

Because Snapchat doesn't offer much in the way of analytics (unless you are using Snapchat for paid advertising), the only way Dutch's team was able to attribute that increase in orders to Snapchat was because of the unique discount code — so keep that in mind when you're creating Stories of your own.

10. HubSpot

While there are a lot of B2C brands doing cool things with Snapchat, there are far fewer B2B companies that have successfully built a following. This is a challenge they wanted to take on at HubSpot, which is why they launched our Snapchat channel in March 2016.

To make our Snapchat channel valuable, they use it to serve as both as a marketing and a recruiting channel — — a place where they can showcase unique culture and perks, awesome employees, and the inbound philosophy.

On the marketing side, they like to give followers a good look inside the company and showcase their culture. The goal here is to be educational, informative, and lovable, which are very familiar goals on their marketing team.

For example, when BuzzFeed News Editor Rachel Zarrell came to HubSpot a few weeks ago to speak about viral content, they showcased some of her talk —

– and what employees thought about it afterward — on Snapchat.

On the culture side, they want to position HubSpot as a destination — and hopefully spur viewers to check out other online offers like their blog, website, careers page, and so on. The key for us is using a human voice that fits in the Snapchat world, rather than a voice that's stuffy or ultra-professional.

11. The Kardashians

The Kardashians came to stardom as a result of their hit reality series," Keeping up with Kardashians". After a constant rise to supremacy, especially through the questionable means of Kim Kardashian, right now the Kardashians are held as the queen of social media usage. They rank among the highly followed people on Snapchat and have used it effectively to market their commercial products. Whether they may be make-up kits, mobile games, emoji stickers, shoes or designer dresses. They have mastered the skill of Social Media Marketing, and analysts have revealed that their sales promotion can solely be as a result of their Snapchat Marketing.

From promos, exhibitions, background reveals, early showcases, they know how to promote their products, With Kim promoting her emoji jewelry and stickers, to

Kylie showcasing the unique colors of her lipstick line and Kendall providing sneak peaks to her photo shoots. Kim has also used her platform to promote her husband's Yeezy Fashion line, concert tickets and music labels. A person looking to promote their products can have a look at their Social Media activity.

Conclusion

I hope this book was able to enlighten you with marketing awareness regarding Social Marketing and its influence in Social Media while providing a successful basis and instep for business promotion. I hope this book also served a vital guideline to promote business though the means of Snapchat, as it renders many business and economical perks through marketing in this platform.

In addition, I hope I shed light on the power of social media marketing and its uses. Once again, thanks again for downloading this book. On the final pages of this book you'll find a BONUS preview of my new newest book, SEO For Beginners to 10x Web Traffic Overnight. Lastly, you'll find my author page and a full list of my books.

Preview of "SEO For Beginners: Simple SEO Strategies to 10x Web Traffic Overnight and Instantly Optimize Visibility on Top Search Engines Google, Bing and Yahoo" by Tony Robson

Chapter 2 - SEO Operation

What are search engines looking for?

When it comes time to optimize SEO for a website, a user must know the virtues of the operation an SEO tool may possess. Hence, it is important for beginners looking to integrate SEO to be equipped with knowledge behind each operating skill:

1) Relevancy

Search engines try to provide the most relevant results to a searcher's query, whether it's a simple answer to the question "how old is Ryan Gosling?" to more complicated queries such as "what is the best steak restaurant near me?" How search engines provide these results is down to their own internal algorithms, which we'll probably never truly determine, but there are factors that you can be certain will influence these results and they're all based around relevancy... For instance: a searcher's location, their search history, time of day/year, etc.

2) Quality of Content

Do you regularly publish helpful, useful articles, videos or other types of media that are popular and well produced? Do you write for actual human beings rather than the search engine itself? Latest research from Searchmetrics on ranking factors indicates that Google is moving further towards longer-form content that understands a visitor's intention, instead of using keywords based on popular search queries to create content.

It's amazing how simply focusing on the user experience will improve the rankings of a website. You can't put lipstick on a pig, as they say (no offense, pigs).

3) User experience

There are many SEO benefits for providing the best possible user experience. An easily navigable, clearly searchable site with relevant internal linking and related content. The goal is to keep visitors on your webpage and hungry to explore further.

4) Site speed

How quickly a website loads is increasingly becoming a differentiator for search engines. Google may soon start labeling results that are hosted on Accelerated Mobile Page (AMP) so this could potentially be an issue for many websites moving forward.

5) Cross-device compatibility

Is your website optimized for any given screen size or device? Bear in mind that Google has stated that responsive design is its preferred method of mobile optimization.

6) Internal linking

We've talked about the benefits of ensuring your site has clear and easy-to-use navigation, but there's also a practice that editors and writers can carry out when publishing articles to help push traffic around the site and that may lead to higher trust signals for Google: internal linking. (See what we did there.)

Internal linking has many advantages:

It provides your audience with further reading options. As long as they're relevant and you use clear anchor text (the clickable highlighted words in any give link). This can help reduce your bounce rates.

It helps to improve your ranking for certain keywords. If we want this article to rank for the term 'SEO basics' then we can begin linking to it from other posts using variations of similar anchor text. This tells

Google that this post is relevant to people searching for 'SEO basics'. Some experts recommend varying your anchor text pointing to the same page as Google may see multiple identical uses as 'suspicious'.

It helps Google crawl and index your site. Those little Googlebots that are sent out to fetch new information on your site will have a better idea of how useful and trustworthy your content is, the more they crawl through your internal links.

7) Authority

An authority website is a site that is trusted by its users, the industry it operates in, as well as other websites and search engines. Traditionally, a link from an authority website is very valuable, as it's seen as a vote of confidence. The more of these you have, and the higher quality content you produce, the more likely your own site will become an authority too. However, as the Search metric research suggests, year–on–year correlations between backlinks and rankings are decreasing, so perhaps over time 'links' may not be as important to SEO as we once thought. There's a good argument raging in the comments to this recent piece on links as a marketing KPI, which offers some diverse views on the subject.

More from Tony Robson:

Hello readers! This is Tony Robson. If you enjoyed this book and are interested in reading more of my work, feel free to click the links below, which will take you directly to the product page on Amazon. All of my books are exclusive to Amazon and are FREE for Kindle Unlimited Members. It is my honor to present to you the following books for your reading pleasure. Enjoy!

SEO For Beginners – Simple SEO Strategies to 10x Web Traffic Overnight and Instantly Optimize Visibility on Top Search Engines Google, Bing and Yahoo

Snapchat Marketing For Business: An Entrepreneur's Guide to Snapchat Marketing Mastery For Business Success!

The Art of the Deal: An Entrepreneur's Guide to Negotiation, Money Management, and Business Success

Mindfulness For Children: The Natural Way to Cure ADHD, Improve Focus and Schoolwork, and Have a Happy and Healthy Child

The Art of Peace and Aikido: An Introduction to The Art of peace and Aikido For Spiritual Awakening

Ketogenic Cookbook: Keto Diet Cookbook with Simple and Delicious Breakfast, Lunch, Dinner, Dessert, and BONUS Smoothie Recipes

Bulletproof Diet Cookbook For Beginners: Quick and Easy Recipes and Smoothies to Lose Fat and Increase Energy

ADHD Diet For Children: Recipes and Diet to Help Your Child Focus, Perform Better at School, and Overcome ADHD For Life

Mindfulness For Beginners: Simple Mindfulness Guide and Mindfulness Meditation Techniques for Stress Reduction and Anxiety Relief

Tooth Decay: Natural Tooth Decay Cure with Simple Treatments to Prevent Tooth Decay For Life

Public Speaking: Overcome Public Speaking Fear and Anxiety For Magic Success and Confidence

Connect with Tony Robson:

Tony Robson Author Page

Tony Robson Facebook Page

Tony Robson Twitter Page

www.ingramcontent.com/pod-product-compliance
Lightning Source LLC
Chambersburg PA
CBHW050013230526
45470CB00003B/948